Contents

What is a mushroom?

A mushroom is a kind of **fungus**. A fungus is like a plant but it has no green leaves. This fungus looks like orange peel!

Spore

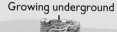
Growing underground

Button mushrooms

Life Cycle of a

Mushroom

Angela Royston

Heinemann
LIBRARY

For more information about Heinemann Library books, or to order, please telephone +44 (0)1865 888066, or send a fax to +44 (0)1865 314091. You can visit our web site at www.heinemann.co.uk

First published in Great Britain by Heinemann Library,
Halley Court, Jordan Hill, Oxford OX2 8EJ
a division of Reed Educational and Professional Publishing Ltd.
Heinemann is a registered trademark of Reed Educational & Professional Publishing Ltd.

OXFORD   MELBOURNE   AUCKLAND
JOHANNESBURG   BLANTYRE   GABORONE
IBADAN   PORTSMOUTH (NH) USA   CHICAGO

Designed by Celia Floyd
Illustrations by Alan Fraser
Printed in China by South China Printing Co. Ltd.

04 03 02 01 00
10 9 8 7 6 5 4 3 2 1

ISBN 0 431 08389 4

British Library Cataloguing in Publication Data

Royston, Angela
  Life cycle of a mushroom
  1. Mushrooms – Life cycles – Juvenile literature
  I. Title   II. Mushrooms
  579.6

Acknowledgements

The Publisher would like to thank the following for permission to reproduce photographs:
Ardea London: David Dixon p.21, DW Greenslade p.4; Bruce Coleman Collection: Hans Reinhard p.12; FLPA: AJ Roberts p.25, E&D Hosking p.11, p.18, John Hawkins p.16, Roger Wilmshurst p.20; Heather Angel: p.15, p.23; NHPA: p.13, GI Bernard p.26, Stephen Dalton p.8; Oxford Scientific Films: Barrie Watts p.9, David M Dennis p.19, GI Bernard p.5, p.6, p.10, p.27, Robin Redfern p.24; Tony Stone: Laurie Campbell p.14; Wildlife Matters: p.7, p.17, p.22.

Cover photograph reproduced with the permission of NHPA

Every effort has been made to contact copyright holders of any material reproduced in this book. Any omissions will be rectified in subsequent printings if notice is given to the Publisher.

There are thousands of different kinds of fungi. This book is about a field mushroom, one of the few kinds of mushroom that you can eat.

2 days later

Ripe mushrooms

5 years

A small beginning

Like all kinds of **fungi**, mushrooms begin life as tiny **spores** in autumn. The spores grow on the underside of the parent mushroom.

Spore

Growing underground

Button mushrooms

Millions of spores blow away from the parent mushroom. Some of the spores land on the moist **soil** in this damp, grassy field.

2 days later

Ripe mushrooms

5 years

Growing underground

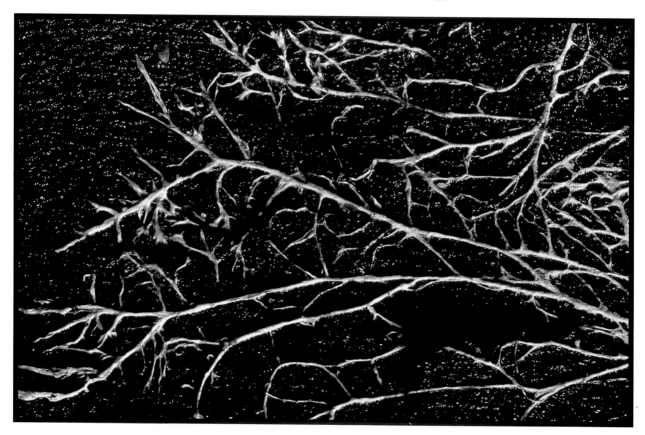

A tiny **thread** grows out from the **spore**. The thread grows longer and longer. It branches into several new threads.

Spore   Growing underground   Button mushrooms

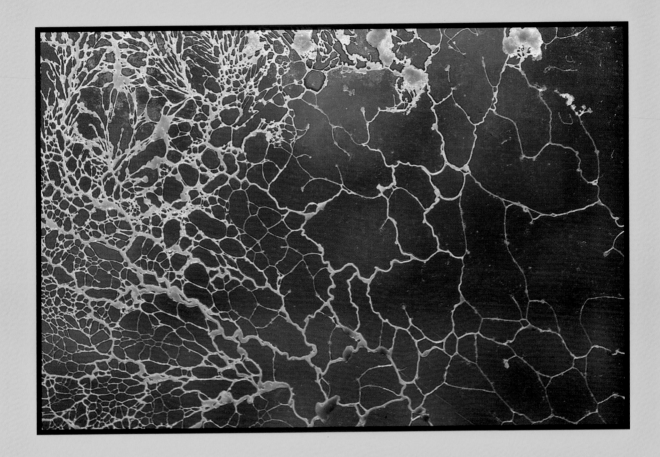

The threads take in food and **nutrients** from the **soil**. Some of the threads join together with threads from other spores.

2 days later

Ripe mushrooms

5 years

The next 12 months

It is late summer and the **soil** is warm and damp. A small mushroom begins to grow underground on part of the web of **threads**.

Spore

Growing underground

Button mushrooms

Other mushrooms are growing too. They all live on the food and water taken in by the threads.

2 days later   Ripe mushrooms   5 years

Growing in the field

As the button mushrooms grow bigger, the **stalks** push up through the **soil**. The top of the mushroom is called the cap.

Spore

Growing underground

Button mushrooms

The cap opens up, like an umbrella.
Can you see the ring of thin skin
where the cap was joined to
the stalk?

2 days later

Ripe mushrooms

5 years

Food for animals

Some of the mushrooms are eaten by animals. Pigs love mushrooms and so does this hungry fox!

Spore

Growing underground

Button mushrooms

As the fox crosses the field, it smells the mushrooms. It picks one or two and chews them up.

2 days later

Ripe mushrooms

5 years

Next day

People like to eat mushrooms too.
Do not pick mushrooms you find
growing **wild** because they might
be **poisonous**.

Spore

Growing underground

Button mushrooms

This woman is an expert. She knows which mushrooms are safe to pick and then she sells them.

2 days later

Ripe mushrooms

5 years

New spores

The underside of the mushroom cap is covered with thin ridges called **gills**. The gills are covered with millions of **spores**.

Spore

Growing underground

Button mushrooms

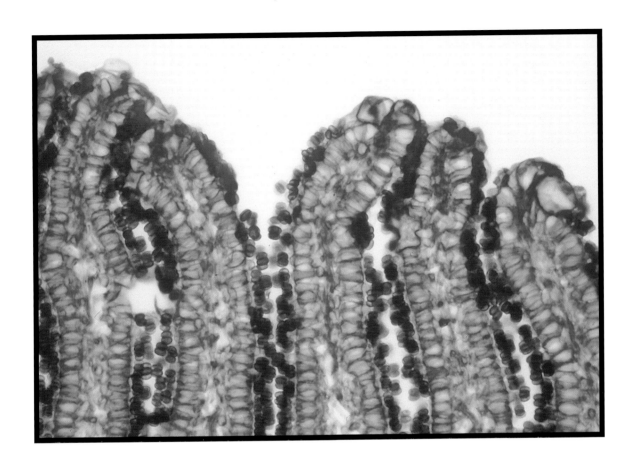

The spores are made inside special
cells along the tips of the gills.
After the spores are carried away
in the wind, the mushroom dies.

2 days later   Ripe mushrooms   5 years

1 day later

Sometimes the wind can blow **spores** a long way. Some spores from the field mushroom ended up in this wood.

Spore

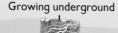
Growing underground

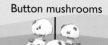
Button mushrooms

Many kinds of **fungi**, such as this honey fungus, grow in the wood. But the **soil** in the wood is not right for the field mushroom. Its spores will not grow there.

2 days later   Ripe mushrooms   5 years

I year later

Some field mushroom **spores** fell in this wet, grassy field. They grew and made new mushrooms.

Spore

Growing underground

Button mushrooms

The **threads** in the old field made new mushrooms too. In late summer the new mushrooms pushed up through the ground.

2 days later

Ripe mushrooms

5 years

5 years later

Every year the underground **threads** grow to make new mushrooms. These field mushrooms have spread out to make a "fairy ring".

Spore

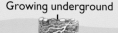
Growing underground

Button mushrooms

A tractor is ploughing up the field. As the soil is broken up and turned over, the threads of all the **fungi** are destroyed.

2 days later

Ripe mushrooms

5 years

A mushroom farm

Most of the mushrooms we eat are grown on special mushroom farms. Unlike other plants, mushrooms do not need light to grow.

Spore

Growing underground

Button mushrooms

These mushrooms are growing in underground caves. It is like autumn all year round here, so new mushrooms grow all the time.

2 days later

Ripe mushrooms

5 years

Life Cycle

Spore

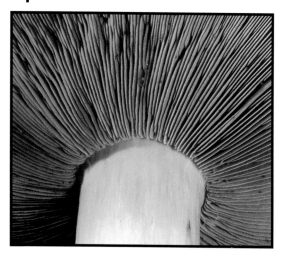

Growing underground

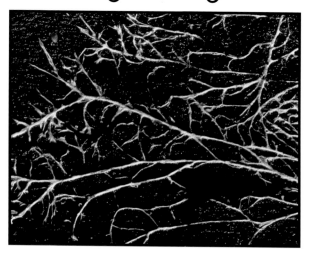

Button mushroom

2 days later

Ripe mushrooms

5 years later

Fact file

There are about 3300 different kinds of mushroom.

Each mushroom produces up to 40 million **spores** every hour for about two days. Only a few of these will grow into new mushrooms.

A few kinds of mushrooms are so **poisonous** they can kill you if you eat them, so do not pick **wild** mushrooms.

Long ago, people used to think that "fairy rings" were made by fairies dancing and that the mushroom were seats the fairies sat on to rest.

Glossary

cells   the tiny building blocks of living things

fungus   a living thing which is like a plant but which cannot make food for itself as green plants can

gills   the ribbed underside of a mushroom

nutrients   chemicals that living things need to be healthy

poisonous   may cause illness or death

soil   the layer of mud which covers much of the land

spores   cells which can grow into new plants or fungi

stalk   stem which joins a flower or fruit to the rest of the plant or the cap of a mushroom to its underground threads

thread   a fine strand, like a hair

wild   growing or living without the help of people

Index